The Hartford Book

CLEVELAND STATE UNIVERSITY POETRY CENTER
NEW POETRY

Michael Dumanis, Series Editor

Samuel Amadon, *The Hartford Book*
John Bradley, *You Don't Know What You Don't Know*
Lily Brown, *Rust or Go Missing*
Elyse Fenton, *Clamor*
Emily Kendal Frey, *The Grief Performance*
Dora Malech, *Say So*
Shane McCrae, *Mule*
Helena Mesa, *Horse Dance Underwater*
Philip Metres, *To See the Earth*
Zach Savich, *The Firestorm*
Sandra Simonds, *Mother Was a Tragic Girl*
S. E. Smith, *I Live in a Hut*
Mathias Svalina, *Destruction Myth*
Allison Titus, *Sum of Every Lost Ship*
Liz Waldner, *Trust*
Allison Benis White, *Self-Portrait with Crayon*
Jon Woodward, *Uncanny Valley*

For a complete listing of titles please visit
www.csuohio.edu/poetrycenter

The Hartford Book

poems

Samuel Amadon

Cleveland State University Poetry Center
Cleveland, Ohio

Copyright © 2012 by Samuel Amadon
All rights reserved
Printed in the United States of America
Printed on acid-free paper

ISBN 978-1-880834-97-8

First edition

5 4 3 2 1

This book is published by Cleveland State University Poetry Center,
2121 Euclid Avenue, Cleveland, Ohio 44115-2214
www.csuohio.edu/poetrycenter
and is distributed by SPD/Small Press Distribution, Inc.
www.spdbooks.org.

Cover image: *Couple kissing, Motherwell,* Oil on board, 2007, by Spencer Lewis.
Used with Permission.

The Hartford Book was designed and typeset by Amy Freels in Mrs. Eaves.

LIBRARY OF CONGRESS CATALOGING-IN-PUBLICATION DATA
Amadon, Samuel.
 The Hartford book : poems / Samuel Amadon.
 p. cm. — (New poetry)
 ISBN 978-1-880834-97-8 (acid-free paper)
 I. Title.

PS3601.M33H37 2011
811'.6—DC23

2011044738

Acknowledgments

Grateful acknowledgement to the editors of journals where versions of the following poems first appeared.

American Letters & Commentary	"The One Person That Winter Who Said I Love You"
The Canary	"Consequences" "Other People's Cars"
Massachusetts Review	"Barbour Street"
Notre Dame Review	"No News Is the News I Need"
Painted Bride Quarterly	"Everyone I Ever Knew from Pittsburgh" "Fall Is for Football, Winter for Hockey"
Southeast Review	"Evergreen Avenue"
Washington Square	"Weather & Happiness"
Western Humanities Review	"Pretty Boys" "The Shit We're Born Into" "Wells"

Thanks to everyone who read versions of these poems over the years, especially: Dean and Carolyn Amadon, Chuck Carlise, Timothy Donnelly, Ryler Dustin, Shafer Hall, Richard Howard, Thomas Hummel, Eric Kocher, Daniel Malakoff, Billy Merrell, Daniel Nester, Jason Nickerson, Michael Schiavo, Emmett Tracy, Dean Young, and most especially: Liz Countryman, whose insight and support were essential in revising this book.

All characters appearing in this work are fictitious. Any resemblance to real persons, living or dead, is purely coincidental.

For my teachers
Richard Howard
& Jack Gethen

Contents

The One Person That Winter Who Said I Love You   1

ONE

Asylum Avenue   5
Wells   8
The Shit We're Born Into   10
Fall Is for Football, Winter for Hockey   12
Homestead Avenue   14
Colt   16
Pretty Boys   18
Cold Fiction   19
Barbour Street   21

TWO

Vanity, Vanity   25

THREE

No News Is the News I Need   39
Consequences   41
Everyone I Ever Knew from Pittsburgh   43
Don't Forget the Horns   45
How My Neighbors Know Me   48
Weather & Happiness   51
Road Conditions Difficult   53
Evergreen Avenue   55
Other People's Cars   57

The Hartford Book

The One Person That Winter Who Said I Love You

When our landlords bought the building,
Kenny said, our apartment had a crackhead
hiding in it & as they walked in he was lighting

a cigarette off the flame of a gas space-heater.
Also, he said our apartment had had dead bodies.
When I was in college I lived in the hotel

where Eugene O'Neil died, on the floor
where Eugene O'Neil died & when
I lived with my parents & my dog died

I slept next to the cardboard box
full of her ashes for fourteen months before I
noticed & when my father poured my

great-grandmother in the bay part of her flew
back toward me in the wind
& I accidentally swallowed her & when

my grandfather was dying I held his hand
& he thought I was my father
& it smelled like a hospital though it

wasn't & the other Alzheimer patients kept coming
in the room & watching us & when
my friend Jack died (car/tree) I met this guy Jesse

at the funeral & when Jesse
died I thought I don't much care if I live
in a house full of dead crack-heads & when

Kenny told me he loved me I told him to hold still
because I had to dab a napkin at
the cut in his scalp where our friend

Sully had stabbed him minutes before.

ONE

Asylum Avenue

My mother says Asylum Avenue's
the wrong place to start
because the neighborhood's still

too nice which makes me think
my mother hasn't been
paying attention & doesn't know

what drug dealers look like
& hasn't walked home
on Asylum from downtown

at two a.m. so drunk she fell down
every time she came across
a curb while dragging with her

the crackhead who started to shake
her hand three blocks back
& won't stop. Or maybe she just

hasn't learned nothing in Hartford
is what it used to be
or where it used to be like the Asylum

Asylum was named for isn't even in
Hartford anymore & was
actually a school for the deaf

& never had any crazy people in it
unlike Hartford where
I can say I've lived a long time

& I've known a lot of different
people & not one
of them is even a little bit sane

so if I was smart I would watch
what I said about them
but I'm not smart & like everyone

else in Hartford I really don't give
a shit. Who would
after all these years of who knows

how much crap we've walked through
like me in that hospital on Asylum
where I was born two months early

& probably should've died but didn't
which makes me feel a little
like my friend Brass who died once

because he's a diabetic & drank too much
& when the EMT brought
him back he punched the guy in the face

& kept drinking & hasn't died again
as far as I know but what
the hell do I know, I'm gone & not

going back & the only time now I come
across the word Hartford is
when I look it up on the internet to see

who Colt & Clemens used to be before
they became apartment
complexes. Or Adrien the Dutch captain

who's just gotten a development named
after him because he landed
here & started this shit but I guess now

he's been dead long enough that he'll
never have to answer for
it which makes him like us because

we never own up to much more than
being from Hartford
which is something no one from

Hartford would ever deny because
though we're all fucked
we've all been fucked before & for

so long that unlike the rest of you
we'd have to be crazy not
to know by now what to expect next.

Wells

In Bushnell Park there are only a couple
      of statues & while I knew
who Minerva was I wasn't sure
      about Horace Wells & I wanted
to know because the plaque underneath
      him says *The Discoverer of*
something I couldn't see & I didn't
      think anyone in Hartford
had ever discovered anything except
      for guns & drugs & when I looked
him up I found out I was
      right because the thing Horace Wells
discovered was anesthesia at some
      kind of show where
a bunch of people inhaled nitrous
      on stage & then ran around like idiots
& when one of them hurt his leg
      he kept running & seemed to feel
nothing & Wells who was a dentist
      thought maybe he could use this
so he got some nitrous & put himself
      under & had a tooth pulled without
any pain, which he thought
      would make him famous so he went
to Boston to put on an exhibition
      & called someone out
of the crowd to go under but
      the man didn't breathe from the bag
long enough & felt
      Wells pull & screamed & everyone
heard it & no one else would volunteer
      & no one wanted to believe
Wells except for William Morton
      who stole the idea using ether instead
of nitrous & got patients
      & patents & a job at Harvard & maybe
Wells never knew it but credit in the books
      goes to Morton or maybe he did
know it because Wells sold his practice

        & left his wife & went to New York
where he went mad & went to jail
        for throwing sulfuric acid at prostitutes
& in his cell inhaled chloroform from
        a rag & cut open his groin vein
& died & the only people now who think
        he discovered anything are some people
in Hartford who can't read
        the sign & probably don't care what it is.

The Shit We're Born Into

When we come into the world first thing
      we shit. At least that's what
Ian says since that's what he did
      but he shit while still in the birth canal
where he was stuck & choked
      to death on it which even after
they brought him back was a hell of a way
      to start life. I don't know
if I shit since I was two months early
      & my parents' stories are usually about me
not being able to breathe
      or having double-hernia surgery. Okie
was that early too but he didn't stay
      in the hospital. When his father
told him he took him home & nursed
      him back to health himself, Okie said
Asshole. The big difference
      between our fathers is mine is a real-
estate appraiser & the son of a radio
      & television host in Wellesley
& Okie's dad is an accountant who
      fought on the wrong side of a war
in Nigeria & has killed
      sixteen people. When Okie would come
home past curfew in high school
      his dad would make him
dig a hole in their backyard
      for three hours & when he finished
he'd make him fill
      the hole. When I fucked up
I had to go to my room where I talked
      on the internet to old men
pretending to be girls my age.
      I don't mind liars as long as they don't
stop lying like Kenny
      who won't let the fake cancer
die. I don't know how he was born but
      when I told him about

Okie's dad he told me his father did
      three voluntary terms in Vietnam
& has killed way more than
      sixteen people & now works for the DEA
which must have something to do with
      Kenny & cocaine & why
when I asked him for the money
      he owed me, he told me about his
colon. I moved back to help
      with the chemo he wasn't going through
& radiation burns he didn't have. I hold
      his hand at night while
he tells me how his oncologist called
      at the club & said he has three months
to live unless he gets
      the colostomy bag. But he won't
get the bag because it's not his style
      & style is all he has
left. I tell him he should but I don't
      push since he doesn't really have
cancer & he's too old
      for his own shit to kill him.

Fall Is for Football, Winter for Hockey

The first time my parents caught me
      lying, it was summer
& I told them I was sleeping at
      Spencer's when I really slept in a car
parked in a field next to
      the leftovers of a bonfire & woke up
to a bee flying into my forehead over
      & over. My mom called
Spencer's house to tell me the girl
      I had a crush on was looking for me
& Spencer's mom said
      we had gone out & weren't coming
back. By August I was sick of lying so I
      admitted I'd started drinking
& then ran out of the house & hopped
      over a neighbor's fence. The neighbor
came out & I called her
      a cunt & she said she'd call the police
but my mom drove up the driveway
      in her pickup & I went home.
My parents thought they'd keep me safe
      by sticking me in a private school
but Hartford works its way in
      no matter what you learn & this winter
I've come to know the worst people
      the city has in it. Kenny
went to wrestle Sully on my birthday
      & I said I'd help but Dicky grabbed
me & I ended up on my face
      with my shirt pulled over my head
like a hockey jersey & my boss saying
      Don't feel bad buddy. You just got
pinned by one of the top fighters in the NHL.
      I never thought I'd know pro-athletes
but I do & they're just as bad
      as you'd expect them to be. What happens
when you give a bipolar Canadian
      two million dollars for a broken
knee & tell him he can never skate
      again? A lot of windows get broken.

He gives himself a black eye
      whenever anyone tells him he can't.
He gets naked in the club & swirls
      his cock around over a crowd
& when he gets kicked out he comes
      over to my house to break another
window. He's not the only one.
      Everyone around here's a pro, even
the bouncer who got picked up by
      the Jets for a week of
preseason & who went to my school
      & once in practice I blew him off
the line but he's a lot bigger now
      so I don't mention it & I don't invite
him over either since I figure I already
      have enough at home
to be afraid of. One morning
      I took a hand poll of who in our
living room had gone to
      private school & all six of them
raised their hands but when I asked
      who was doing crystal-meth
right now they were so excited by
      the question they set the crystal down
so everyone could raise
      both hands. It's snowing tonight
& my roommate who claims
      he could've played
for the Whalers if they hadn't left
      town & he hadn't become a drug
dealer wakes me up & wants
      to borrow my car to make some
money skidding it around town
      on the ice. It's easier to say
yes so I say it though I know
      I'll spend the whole time he's gone
watching for the car
      out the window where the snow
won't stop falling as maybe it always
      seems it won't though
the way this winter's been going
      there's reason to think the seasons
are a little longer now
      than what they used to be.

Homestead Avenue

The first winter I came back home
I worked for my father
taking pictures of commercial

properties all over the state which
meant I spent the day
stuck in traffic & hating it & so

I started to find new ways of getting
around & began to take
Homestead on my way home

from the office to avoid rush hour
in Hartford which is made up
entirely of people who don't live

in Hartford & who get on the highway
as quick as they can & have no
reason to take a road like Homestead

which goes nowhere but Hartford
& I'm pretty sure even if
they did need to go down it they'd

find another way not wanting to see
any of this shit like
bulletproof liquor stores or boarded-up

warehouses or crackheads on bicycles
or the hand-painted sign
for an exterminator which reads *BE SAFE*

LEAVE THE KILLING TO US.
I think Homestead's where
the lot for the fish market used to be

but I'm not sure how to remember
what was where when
landmarks keep disappearing, plus

it's harder for me to say where
the fish market was since
every time we went there to buy

weed in high school I was hidden
under a blanket in the back
of my own car because white people

were never allowed to buy anything
at the fish market & I can't
pretend I'm Puerto Rican like some

people can. But I was there & I knew
how it worked like a drive-thru
with a line of cars in one side of the lot

to meet the first in a line of dealers
who came up to your window
& took your order & gave you what you

wanted & on you went into the line
of cars going out
the other side. The fish market's

been closed for years now, which means
there must be some lot
somewhere else in the city where

the same sort of thing is happening
but I don't smoke weed now
& knowing where a place like that is

gets a lot harder when you aren't in
high school & I guess I miss
knowing things I'm not supposed to

& I miss driving places for some
reason which doesn't stop
me from driving around for no reason

except to maybe remember what
happened on some night
when life felt a little more interesting.

Colt

No one makes guns in the Colt
        gun factory anymore instead
they make art. I went on a blind
        date with a fat girl who lived there
& didn't make anything
        except comments about how
much head was on her beer
        & I hated her immediately
which didn't stop me from
        suggesting she take me
to the movies after she paid my tab.
        I passed out during the third
preview & woke up
        later with my fingers wedged
between her thighs. I've never been
        the best date. I tend to lie
about myself & fake sleep like
        in Kindergarten the first time
I kissed a girl when
        Kirsten Sichler slid over to my mat
& said *Ben?* & I said *yes* because
        even though that wasn't
my name it could've been & I wanted
        to kiss her & I've done a lot more
lying over the years
        & probably will still unless
I start listening to my roommate
        when he says *At least drugs
never make me buy them dinner*
        which reminds me how I used to
think when I hung around
        with people like Legend smoked
his dust-blunts (maple leaves
        soaked in formaldehyde)
& watched him punch slow-moving
        cars with no fear of the cops
coming down the street. This
        was when I didn't have any money

for gas or anything to do but
  stand around at night
with kids in parking lots until someone
  pointed an unloaded gun at me
& said *Boom* & I believed
  him & Legend shot himself & I
decided that was enough. But
  then the cops said Legend
didn't kill himself someone shot him
  & some money disappeared
which meant someone was
  lying & we thought it was Amir
who the week I let him stay
  at my house stole
my parents' VCR while I was
  busy on the floor with the lights
down making out with some
  girl whose name I can't remember.

Pretty Boys

Brass owes a whole bunch of coke dealers
       a whole bunch of money
so he's been locked up in a motel room
       with his mom who's only fifteen years
older than him. My punching bag
       is in there which is too bad because
tonight I really would like to punch
       something. His pit bull Enzo is
there too. I really like Enzo & I've put
       my fist in his open jaw. The bartender
I work for is also named
       Enzo but I don't get to put my fist in
his mouth. He's half-Greek & half-
       Italian, which my roommate
says is so Mediterranean that his
       nut must taste like olive oil. He is
very good looking as is his
       best friend & after Enzo got in a fight
they both checked first thing
       the perfection of his
face. Sometimes when I'm at work
       I hope Brass will walk out of the crowd
in the purple club light. He doesn't
       come to places like this & he can't
come back to Hartford but he was
       funny & I remember some
of the things he said like *I'm going*
       outside for a minute where we watched
him for an hour shaking
       in the cold by the high metal fence
in our backyard waiting there
       for something or
someone who wasn't going to come.

Cold Fiction

Even my dad knows Mitchell
    & if he saw him walking his dogs
down Evergreen I bet he'd yell out
    like I do & be happy to stop
in the cold for a bit, holding the sides
    of a hot cup of coffee the smell of
which makes Mitchell's blind pitbull
    snap. This winter is twice as cold
as I remember the winter could be
    & you can tell Mitchell's
a little off since he's repeating himself
    & keeps telling me about his friend
who pretended to go to
    the University of Hawaii by hiding
in his basement all winter & spending
    what money he had on sessions
at the tanning salon. Mitchell wants
    to know if I think Kenny's really got
cancer & I say I don't know
    though I do know he's really got a drug
problem but I try not to get too far into it
    because as much as I think
I'm leaving Hartford I'm sure Kenny
    isn't & I don't want to bad-mouth him
to Mitchell since Mitchell's
    the one thing Hartford's got.
Mitchell says he's miserable because
    the junkie who's been
screwing the chick upstairs takes
    ten to fifteen long showers a day
& the building's so fucked
    that all this shitty water's pouring
from the ceiling & even after he takes
    buckets of it & dumps
them on the junkie's car he's still
    in a bad mood & it's cold as hell
& he tries reading
    verse but it doesn't help. I know Mitchell's

been cooking at the Prospect
  forever but now he tells me he also
used to work in some bookstore
  on Albany Avenue twenty years
ago when it was a different Albany
  Avenue & once when the Russian
Ballet came into town
  they came into his store & asked
if he had *American* poetry while
  nodding to their escorts
in the corner & he slipped one
  the address of the Prospect & when
she showed he lent her poets
  she'd never heard of *Mandelstam
Tsvetaeva Akhmatova* & she promised to
  but never returned
them & he got in some trouble.
  Never mind that he says he wishes
he could introduce me to
  William Meredith who once read
Mitchell's poems & liked some
  but is dead now so that's no
help & I tell him Meredith's not dead
  I met him last summer & talked
to him about Connecticut
  but Mitchell's not listening
& it doesn't matter anyway
  since we're both freezing
& even the dogs want to go in.

Barbour Street

My junior year of high school I had
to go all spring to this
middle school on Barbour Street

for an afterschool thing for college
applications or whatever
& I tried to look like I wanted to

be there but those kids knew I didn't
& they could see I didn't know
shit about them or their neighborhood

so it's not surprising they didn't wave
that summer when Spencer
& I rode past them day after day

on the way to the gym where we were
getting ready for football
season or fucking off on our bikes

& Spencer kept pointing out to me
how even though a block
out there was about twice as long

as my block instead of there being
three hydrants evenly placed
along it there was only one at the end

of each so there had better not
be any fires in the middle
of those streets which I would think

about the summer I was back from
school when I'd drive
Ray Rose home from work at this

Italian restaurant where Kenny got
me a job. Ray had a tear
tatooed by his eye & somebody had

told me by then what that meant
so I never said no to him
& every night I got to be the white kid

in the North End past dark parked
on the edge of some huge
project waiting for Ray to finish

whatever lesson from jail he was
teaching me since
everyone from jail always has some

endless lesson they want to teach
& so I learned a little
more about the ghetto than I was

supposed to & I kept Ray friendly
& even got the chance to
teach him something I'd just learned

about Hartford which was that there
used to be a field where
his mom lives now & when the circus

came to town they put up these tents
which were rainproofed in
gasoline & then all these people died

in a fire which it turns out is actually
the first thing after
insurance Hartford is famous for.

TWO

Vanity, Vanity

If Myles Standish had his way I never
would've been born
& Longfellow never would've written

his poem about how my great-great-
however-many-greats-
grandfather John Alden stole Priscilla

Mullins from Standish but Longfellow
wouldn't have been born
either since he was related to John

& Priscilla too & he never would've
been too late to put out
his first wife when she caught

fire sealing envelopes for him
& never would've translated
the Inferno trying to get over her

but I bet someone else would've
& I bet someone sort of like
me would've been born & in Hartford

& had the same trouble I've had
leaving Hartford because
everyone in Hartford has a hard time

imagining anywhere else since
none of us read very much
& no one anywhere else thinks

very much of us & anyway I don't
know anyone with
a car that could make it over a hill

out of Hartford & if most people
are like me they have
too many enemies at the bus

station to try Greyhound so everybody
stays & lives in apartments
with mustaches over their doorways

in buildings named things like
Clemens Court or *The Twain
Complex* though I doubt many people

who live in those buildings care that
they're named for the same
person or that he'd been to places

with rivers named something
other than Connecticut
& the one time I reread *Huck Finn*

I thought even if we could get
a raft built the only
place it'd take us is to sea & I'd

put money on us not making it
across the Atlantic or even
to Plymouth where if I decided

to steal my roommate's girl like
John Alden I'm sure
he wouldn't react like Standish

& say something like *I alone am
to blame for mine was folly*
I mean those words weren't

the ones on his lips the time
he found me & her
in a dark room with candles

burning, listening to the bad R&B
our downstairs neighbors
never turn off & we probably

would've had to hold off Thanksgiving
for a year if he hadn't believed me
when I said we were trying to

conjure the crackheads whose bodies
were found lying on
our living room floor before we

moved in which might've bugged
me if it weren't for all these
stories I can hear myself repeating,

how I was seven & my father poured
my great-grandmother into
the bay & her ashes flew back

at me in the wind & I swallowed her
or if I hadn't slept with
the cardboard box where my parents

left the remains of my dog Twyla
Tharp behind my head
for fourteen months before I

noticed & you know when I went to
college I lived in the hotel
where Eugene O'Neil died

on the floor where Eugene O'Neil
died & I used to be
convinced that he'd come to me

while I was sleeping & whisper
all kinds of shit like *the only
ears that can ever hear one's secrets

are one's own* which was a lot more
fucked up than anything
those dead crackheads ever

would've said & as for Kenny's
girlfriend I wasn't doing
anything with her & didn't ever

want to but still he made me
nervous after that
& I made sure I never

paid her any pilgrim compliments
like *I see you spinning & spinning
never idle a moment but thrifty & thoughtful*

of others which really wasn't that hard
not to say out loud but still
it was safer for me to spend time

in bars where no one listens to
anything I shouldn't say
or cares about any of my facts

like our Old State House is the Oldest
Old State House in New England
or that we have the First Housing Project

in the Country & they don't mind
that we lost Insurance Capital
of America to India or that we made

up for that by taking Most Crackheads
Per Capita away from
Lowell & nobody's ever impressed

that *The Hartford Courant* is the Nation's
Oldest Continuously Published
Newspaper or that once they gave me

sixty dollars for writing about why
underage kids should get to
drink more & the one thing anyone

says when I mention attending
the Second Largest Private
University in the U.S. is *What the fuck*

you do that for? & I say *To get the fuck
out of Hartford* but having
come back I sound pretty stupid

saying that & try to come up with
better answers for my
college friends when they ask why

I'm living down here like *it's so cheap*
or *you can't get arrested for anything* or
everyone I know works in a bar which

was what I kept telling my friend Jack
trying to get him to move
here instead of Florida where he went

with his girlfriend & got a job baking
pastries while she studied
to become a veterinarian & lived in

a little house with an overgrown lawn
that she wouldn't let him
cut in case of rabbits & where I really

meant to visit until he stopped
inviting me after he ran
into a fallen tree with his car on

his way to work at five in the morning
& because the casket was
closed at the wake I never saw

him again though I still see his name
every time I type the letter
J into the address box of my email

because I don't know how to get
the damn program to stop
asking me to write him & I'll start to

sometimes, thinking I'll ask him
how he managed to live
all over the place for years never

paying any rent & usually with no
more of a plan than
driving to San Francisco & walking

into a bar & buying someone a drink
& all I remembered of how
he stayed for free in Boston when

I knew him was something about cooking
food & something about
keeping quiet which are two things

I'll never be any good at & so if Twain's
right & *the unspoken word is
capital* then I'm going to stay one broke

motherfucker since I can't stop talking
& even worse repeating
this stupid history of how I was

born two months early in a hospital on
Asylum the year my uncle
got cancer & I couldn't breathe

& probably should've died but didn't
& he didn't die either until
I was twenty & at his funeral I didn't

know what to say to my kid cousins
who didn't know it wasn't
the right time to call me a drunk

& I didn't really think I should stop
them since they'd hit it
dead on & I didn't know what to say

to my grandmother who knew but
wasn't supposed to know
I was driving straight from the funeral

to Panama City with Jack's roommate
Seth who ended up arrested
down there but got out & got us back

to Boston where my grandfather was
in a little bed dying & I held
his hand & he thought I was my

father & it smelled like a hospital
though it wasn't & the other
Alzheimer patients kept coming

in & staring at us & then another
funeral & afterward
I told everyone I'd decided to

move out to California where
Kenny said he was living
but then I heard he was lying

& still home & I couldn't see why
I shouldn't want to live
in Hartford & so I moved in with him

& his girlfriend three blocks away
from the hospital where
I was born & forgot I'd ever been

anywhere else until Jack's wreck
& I went to Pittsburgh for
the funeral & their family was huge

& I didn't know what to say when
people asked me if I was
a cousin & I slept in Jack's living room

with his pitbull who was old & wanted
to die & whined like
a screen door all night because no one

let him creep out & hide under
bushes like the time Twyla
got out of the basement where

we kept her crippled & incontinent
for a year & I was supposed to
be watching her & I didn't know

what to say to my father when he
came home & I'd lost her like
I lost one of Jack's real cousins after

the funeral & after a handle
of tequila & I walked
around this Pittsburgh street having

forgotten where I was & thinking
it was Asylum though it wasn't,
still I found him & carried him on

my shoulder back to the party
& to his friend Jesse
who stared at you like some

people I know do & so I liked
him for reminding me
of all my screwed up friends

though when I got home & saw
them I moved right away to
Cape Cod to sell books & not guess

every morning how much of my
brain was gone from booze
but I let Jack's cousin & his friend

Jesse come stay with me, which
ended my sober streak just
as it was getting started & I kept

selling books though I never read
any except somehow
the *Inferno* which made me think

I didn't really know that many
dead people until Jesse
killed himself & you know there

was no way I was going to a funeral
for someone I met
at a funeral so I moved home

instead where Kenny told me
he had cancer, which
he didn't & my godfather told us

on Christmas he had lung cancer
& he did & he died
& after that many funerals I wasn't

about to tell Kenny I didn't believe
he was sick even though
I never saw him go to that

hospital on Asylum & I thought
if he does have cancer
at least I have something to drink

about, which I did & plenty & for
four months my life was
nothing but booze & vomit

& waking up on an air mattress
wondering how much of my
brain wasn't coming back though

I knew it was a lot since I couldn't
read a book for more than
five minutes or remember what

fucked-up thing I'd done five days
ago & still I got up
every day & showered & combed

my hair & put back on the same
dirty clothes since I wasn't
trying to impress any guys named

Murder or any of the minor league
hockey players who kept
bleeding in our living room & who

must have impressed all the other
psychos Kenny dragged in
like Nigger Mike who was this big

ass white dude who got his name
from his neighbors down
on Mather Street where he got

robbed every night walking home
from work but still went
to work every day & walked home

every night & one night I woke up
to him in my room offering
me a blunt of angel dust which

I refused & instead offered him
my bat saying *You'd better get
the fuck away from my books* thinking

at the time he was trying to steal
them & he laughed
& said *What the fuck you do that for?*

& left me alone to wonder & I ended
up starting that book of Twain's
about the guy from Connecticut which

I'd never read before & I thought
maybe this one would tell me
the way out but I fell asleep thinking

about this crackhead who I used to
wash dishes with & whose name
was Hercules like the character in

Twain's book who works at the Colt
gun factory & who came into
my dream as both of them at once

swinging a crowbar at my head
& it hurt like hell & as I fell
I wondered when the last time I'd

had a dream was & couldn't say, though
when I woke expecting England
I got more Hartford & Hercules split

& there were no knights & no Merlin
& it didn't seem like Camelot
was near but I went looking for it

anyway & since Twain says Camelot
at first seems like an asylum
I found a group of lunatics who were

trying to move Bushnell Park by
lugging flagstones from
one of its walls & throwing them

through the rear windshields of parked
cars & I hoped they
would head me the right way until

I got close enough to see who they
were & I already knew
each one of them & knew where

they were going & it wasn't to
an asylum since there is
no asylum in Hartford & never

has been since Asylum is named
for the World's First School
for the Deaf which skipped town

years ago & the building where it
was is now part of that
hospital I was born in & where I

figured I might as well go take
a look now since I can't
seem to see anything from anywhere

else anyway & when I got there
I tried to climb the fire
escape & fell & tried again

& didn't fall & got up on the roof
where I was blown around
& had to grab onto a weathervane

spinning & spinning & shrieking
so loud I couldn't hear
Kenny screaming & I couldn't even

hear myself so for once there
wasn't a voice in my ear
telling me anything & I could

see the whole city & you know
I never saw before
every single road is pointed out.

THREE

No News Is the News I Need

The kitchen of the South Green
        firehouse caught on fire
when a pot of water boiled away
        & the cutting-boards left inside
burned while the firemen
        were at a middle school. A parking
attendant called it in but didn't
        speak English & later
explained *He no believe me.* Down on
        Park Street an SUV flipped over
the curb & smacked into
        an apartment building. The woman
inside told reporters *This is the second*
        time this has happened
since we moved here. We need to move
        somewhere else. But no one here ever
moves somewhere else
        & everyone should stay inside
& not answer the door ever even
        for trick-or-treaters who
sometimes carry guns in their costumes
        & shoot people in the face like
Juan Rivera who neighbors
        say *wore baggy jeans but wasn't into*
thuggery. Rivera was only the sixteenth
        killing of the year down
from forty-four last year which
        probably doesn't include the sixteen-
year-old drug dealer who got
        shot by the cops outside my apartment
the week in June when I was
        already kicking myself for
staying in Hartford all summer
        but this year it seems I'm gone & not
coming back except maybe
        for Thanksgiving & I'm already
worried about who I'm going to
        run into that day. It just takes a little

  boredom & a shot with someone
    I shouldn't be shooting with
to start me talking about changing my
    address back. Maybe I'm better off
just reading the *Courant* even if
    the story of some fire makes me
nostalgic for the city & remember that
    other fire where I waited
in traffic outside the burning
    nursing-home & watched snow
falling slowly over
    the elderly piling out into
the street in a long line which
    blocked a stream
of cars that all started honking.

Consequences

Kenny tried to tell me what a bad idea
      it would be to hook up
with Tara but we were taking shots
      of vodka in my kitchen with this
Dominican guy & she reached
      over & pulled my dick out so how
was I going to listen to anyone about
      what was a good idea.
I didn't listen to my friends
      when they said buying a Ford Pinto
from a thrift store with no papers
      & no plates & no brake pads
& a hole in the floor was a stupid
      thing to do. Why would I? The car
only cost two hundred
      dollars & I had two hundred dollars
& I knew I could rip the plates off
      of other people's cars & jam
them onto mine & if I swore I wouldn't
      go over ten miles an hour I didn't really
need brakes. I guess this is just
      the kind of shit I do & so I'll keep
spending days like that one
      where I sat for hours under my living room
table listening to Kenny tell me about
      Tara's boyfriend who's this bouncer
on steroids who carries three guns
      on him at all times. Which isn't to say
I handle it okay. After that thing
      with Tara I called all my friends to say
good-bye & was extra-nice to my mother
      for a few weeks that I spent constantly
checking for a laser dot on my forehead
      until Kenny finally got tired of it & said
Don't worry buddy. I'm not going to let
      anyone shoot you. I believed him.
I mean why not if anyone
      knows about sleeping around it's Kenny

who can't walk to the store without
        cheating on his girlfriend
Lisa who he never calls or visits
        & who never leaves him. So I began
to feel better about
        the whole thing though I didn't sleep
with Tara again for a couple of months
        & when I did it was right
before I left Hartford for the summer
        so when she told me her boyfriend
had broken up with her
        mostly because of me I didn't worry
much. I'm out of there & I didn't
        expect to hear anything
about any of them again though
        I did when Kenny called me to say
he woke up one day & tried
        to be good by surprising Lisa
at her place & found her on the couch
        fucking Tara's three-gun
toting, newly single boyfriend.

Everyone I Ever Knew from Pittsburgh

One of the Pirates got arrested for
        tripping a woman in a hot-dog
suit as she raced down the first base
        line in a contest with a man in
a sausage suit & a man
        in a kielbasa suit during some kind
of seventh-inning-stretch sideshow
        & it made me think of everyone
I had ever known from Pittsburgh
        because it seemed exactly like
the kind of thing that
        one of them would've done. I never
thought any of them were bad
        people but I always knew
they were up to something with their
        pointed faces & their wait-while-I-
think smiles & their walk
        thrust so far forward it looks like
falling. Take Jack who taught me
        you can live anywhere as long
as you make yourself useful & do
        those things the people letting you
live there don't want to have to
        do. A lesson he must have taught
his cousin Malakoff who I let live
        with me one summer
& who fed me every night half
        with the food he found in people's
cupboards & half with
        what he found in the trash & who
used my spare room to build bicycles
        out of parts of other bicycles
he found on the street until he moved
        to D.C. just for the protests & learned
to crawl his way out of riots
        under the bodies of unconscious
women. I even thought of Dave Bouchat
        who wasn't from Pittsburgh

though his family was & who wanted
        to be a racecar driver & used to take me
in his car & launched us over hills
        & land on one tire & never killed anyone
until he joined the Army. They all seem
        like they have a knife somewhere
or have an idea of where to get a knife
        somewhere & while they aren't from
Hartford I think I understand
        their strange lives run by
drugs & engines & the urge to walk
        faster than their legs
which must come from Pittsburgh
        because I've been there & when
I saw the hills people
        were falling down them all the time.

Don't Forget the Horns

Mel's the one black man on Cape Cod
        & my only friend from working at
Blockbuster. He doesn't have a driver's license
        even though he's thirty
so I go over to his house to pick him
        up & get dirty looks from his girlfriend
Shelly's kids, especially
        the five-year-old who's Mel's too
& screams at me. Their mom's too stoned
        to know I'm picking him up
so he can cheat on her but the kids
        get it & I wish he'd let me wait
in the car. He takes forever
        getting ready & brings a bottle of Hennessy
along for the ride. I drop him
        at some bar with some white girl & when
he calls me two days later
        I take him home. We tell Shelly we stayed
at my parents' house but where that is
        changes from Boston to
Brooklyn to Hartford because Mel
        forgets where I'm from & Shelly's too
stoned to know the difference.
        This isn't nearly the first time I've had
to help a friend cheat on a girl.
        When Kenny & the fat girl
who worked at the Colonic Center
        dropped me off at our apartment
I was worried what I was
        going to say to Ken's live-in girlfriend
Lisa who was waiting upstairs to
        interrogate anyone coming in
& I was so drunk I couldn't face her
        so I slipped in the back & went
right to my room where I took all
        my clothes off & lay down on my bed
without a blanket so when
        she came in she didn't want to ask

me questions. Mel's having a party soon
      & he's been handing out fliers
to teenagers who come in the store.
      I don't expect many will show up
because after he tells the guys
      to bring chicks he says if their friends
wile out he's got guns. The party was
      the day after Halloween but I still
managed to find horns & a tail
      for a costume. Every woman
there was a waitress & over
      forty. There were three gypsies & when
I told the one with the worst
      Boston accent *No I've never read Anne*
Rice's novels she said *Well if for whatever*
      reason one of us were to turn
into a vampire, because of her books we'd
      know how to relate to the other vampires.
I couldn't handle the kitchen
      & I was pretty stoned so I went into
the basement where Mel had rented
      two club speakers from
Rent-A-Center (I never knew
      anyone who had ever rented from
Rent-A-Center) & I danced
      alone in the strobe light shaking
my tail's shadow around the wall.
      There was no furniture
so when I passed out I had to
      pass out in a corner & later when I
saw I was lying
      next to a pool of vomit I got
up & crept out the bulkhead
      & climbed into my car
under a pile of garbage
      in the backseat & locked the door.
Mel told me next day
      I left my horns in the vomit
so I didn't get away with doing it
      though I got out
of cleaning it when two weeks
      later Shelly caught Mel cheating

    & he convinced her
           in return that what she couldn't
remember from the party was
        screwing me & so I wasn't
welcome in their house anymore.

How My Neighbors Know Me

When I moved to my dead grandmother's
    house on Cape Cod my mother
asked me to introduce myself to
    the man who lives next door with his
grown-up son who she says
    can't leave the house because he's
strange though in what way she didn't
    explain & I was curious & drove
there intending first thing to drop by
    but then when I got to our house
I found the college girls
    from Western Mass my parents had
rented to for the summer had left
    the place a wreck of dented
walls & vodka bottles & panties.
    It took three days to clean the house
& I forgot about meeting the neighbors
    & weeks went by & it's too late now
after who knows what they've seen
    me do. I must seem a little strange
to them. I keep all my lights on all the time.
    I sit in my car in the driveway
drinking scotch. Who knows how I'd react
    to seeing a grown man chased
around his yard by another grown
    man with a grill lighter
screaming *I'm gonna burn your chest*
    hair off on a work-day no less
which is exactly what
    happened when my friends came
to visit. The neighbors probably
    saw us that first night since
Malakoff's good friend Jesse insisted
    I didn't have to pull the shades
since he was mainlining
    water & not heroin & *just going*
through the motions which is how
    he justified it to me

while Malakoff explained he'd
  brought Jesse to my house to detox
& hadn't told me because
  he didn't think I'd mind which
I did a little later when a whole lot
  of my grandmother's
furniture got broken though I'll admit
  I'd never seen someone detox
& thought the idea was
  funny & said he could stay so
we drank some absinthe & ate some
  painkillers & who really cares
about anything anyway though
  I should have cared about Jesse
mainlining absinthe
  with the front door open or made
him put the needles away when we
  drove over to the bay at two a.m.
where the two of them ran out
  on the flats before I could stop
them & had to chase them
  back before the tide came in.
We lay down on the beach & looked up
  for what felt like a minute
& I said *We can't sleep here* & they said
  But we just got here which was wrong
because that minute had been
  two hours so we left & couldn't find
our way home through rotary after
  rotary until Malakoff
accidentally put us on the right
  road when he saw a supermarket
I wouldn't let him stop at
  because I didn't think this was
a town where you should be jumping
  into supermarket dumpsters
for food at four a.m. which was
  a logic they couldn't understand
but gave in to anyway & we
  got back & slept with the door open
& some leaves got in & Jesse woke up
  first & kicked my mailbox

off its post & then duct-taped it
  back on with half a roll of duct-tape
which he *god bless him*
  thought I wouldn't notice but I did
& laughed & didn't get mad at him
  though it's now an awful
eyesore for the neighbors who don't
  know me or ever tell me that
they don't think that sort of thing is funny.

Weather & Happiness

That time I circled the room asking
      about my happiness I was
told it would be better if I sat
      down. No one tells you when you start
to talk about the weather
      that the weather will end up being
the only thing you have to talk
      about. If I were to
talk about something it would
      probably be how much I have
to drink to stop
      the back pain I get from sleeping
in the places I sleep after drinking
      too much like under
the picnic-table on my parents'
      front porch or under the similar
picnic-table on their
      neighbor's front porch or even once
under a bench on the Brooklyn Bridge.
      I'm kidding. I've never slept
under a bench. But when I woke up
      on that bridge I saw birds & sun
& breeze which made me
      stagger quickly into the subway
where I knew if I didn't say anything
      to the token guy he wouldn't
wake up to stop me from hopping
      the turnstile or making the eight a.m.
bus back to Hartford. There
      was no one in the back of that bus
but me, & one guy who sat down
      in the seat next to me
put a throw rug with a hole cut
      in the middle over his head, took off
his pants & handed
      me a warm Budweiser. Right as I
opened it he went into the restroom
      where he stayed for the next

three hours not disturbing anyone
      except when we hit the hill at
New Haven & liquid
      came down the aisle which bothered
me most of all because by then
      that beer had made me
really need to pee. I don't think
      there's been a day lately where
I didn't wake up bursting
      with piss & I'm pretty sure that like
most everything that is going to
      stay the same except
for all the things that have
      gone & are going to stay missing.
Like breakfast. I never
      have breakfast anymore because
the morning has changed & it's only
      good now for making
myself promises in the shower
      or having a cup of black coffee
leftover from yesterday
      while checking the sky behind
the shade to guess how the day
      will be & what the hell is
the next thing I'll have to say.

Road Conditions Difficult

When I drove over to my godfather's
    house to shovel him out
the road was a sheet of ice & this was
    before I knew how to tap the breaks
so when my car spun
    around a second time I expected
to keep turning while it kept snowing
    which it did the whole time
I shoveled, making me wonder
    what the hell I was doing there,
guessing as I worked which
    shape in the windows was him.
I expected coughing loud enough
    to shake the block. That's not
how it happens. There's diagnosis
    & surgery & when that fails that's it
someone else has
    disappeared. Which doesn't change
how much I need to get my coffee
    from Peter B's where
I used to get my coffee free from
    Blake who's gone but let me sit
last summer in the A.C.
    drinking scotch out of paper cups
like I was doing the night my cell-
    phone kept dying before
I could hear what the people who
    kept calling kept saying. When Kenny
showed up we drove over
    to Doug's house where I dented
the car in front of me drunk-parallel-
    parking & when I told Doug
his house smelled a lot like crap
    he told me to look down at the dog-
shit splattered up my legs.
    My phone rang & I said *Quick
before it dies* & Malakoff told me
    Jack's dead. A tree fell over

   the road in Florida on his way
     to work. Kenny & I went to the bar
where three bartenders cut me
     off & when I went home to sleep
I threw up in bed & slept in it & spent
     the next morning piecing
together Gainesville news I found
     on the internet & vacuuming
the mattress. It took
     hours but if you try hard enough
you can get anything clean. The funeral
     was in Pittsburgh & when
it was over we drank a handle
     of tequila & I had to go looking
for Malakoff who was thirsty
     enough to go for a drink from a hose
in somebody's backyard. I found him
     & struggled with him up
the stairs on my shoulder & we
     wrestled in the living room where I
flipped him over my back
     so we landed on Jack's kid-brother's
girlfriend who didn't get mad though
     it was her apartment
& we were making some mess which
     I never saw since I walked out with
my eyes shut & kept them
     that way & don't remember even
seeing a road sign until New Jersey
     where they say
On Incline Accelerate To Maintain Speed.

Evergreen Avenue

Though I'd never admit it if someone
asked I'm not actually from
Hartford. I grew up in West Hartford

two blocks from the city line
on a nice street in a nice
house with two nice parents & never

lived in Hartford until I came home
after college & moved to
Evergreen Avenue which is only

six blocks east of my parents
& already the city's not
that nice. It's the sort of place

where fuck-ups from my town
settle down to pay two
hundred a month in rent & give up

grassy lawns for yards made of dirt
& glass & sometimes oyster
shells if Kenny & I get wasted & fill

another champagne bucket with
oysters & walk around
shucking them wherever we want

because we don't give a fuck what
the Russian family who cleans
these yards has to pick up. Next door

to us there's a transvestite named Joy
who sells codeine & once
I saw a Pontiac Fiero pull up

onto her yard in the rain & what must
have been a family of eight
climbed out & they must have really

needed some codeine because
they stood there in the rain
for over an hour shouting *Joy! Joy! Joy!*

When I first moved here a group
of old men would sit all day
in these beach chairs by the bus stop

playing spades & talking loud until
they died or moved away
which makes it seem quiet now

& it's the quiet makes me nervous.
Like when I'm walking home
from work at night with a big roll

of money in my pocket I don't
want to be able to hear
an engine turn over in some dark

Honda a hundred yards away which
is why this one night
when all the lights on Evergreen

went out at three in the morning
I was glad that there was
a two-year-old who'd gotten away from

his mother & run into the street because
the only sound you could
hear was that damn kid screaming.

Other People's Cars

I told Kenny I didn't feel comfortable
      having breakfast with him
because I was in graduate school
      now & he was leaving threatening
messages on my voice mail
      before the sun came up & that wasn't
okay with me anymore & he told me
      he had to go to Washington
& he had the Capitol on the other line
      so he hung up & that could've been
the end of us but you know
      Christmas is Christmas so I wound up
home getting lectured by a drug-addict
      about how I let him
down & drinking scotch & trying to get
      a minute alone with his new roommate
who says he saw hospital
      release papers with *colon cancer* on them
so maybe I'm the real asshole or Kenny's
      learned how to forge
but either way he must have lied
      about the Capitol I mean I know
he's a Republican & all
      but what would he & the Leadership
meet for & now he's saying he hates
      Bush so he might actually be
getting sober because I always believed
      the whole right-wing drug-dealer thing
was a byproduct of
      cocaine & I told him my phone number
& he wrote it down backwards & winked
      at me which was one
of the kindest things he's ever
      done. I never really believed much
he told me & only justified
      living with him by figuring even if
the cancer wasn't real he still needs
      some help & it's hard

to explain what it was like living there
        drunk & doubting my own mind
all the time after that morning
        when my car was parked in the space
next to the space where I knew
        I left it & Kenny gave me
my keys & said *I don't know why*
        they were in my pocket & I said *Because*
you took my car, you asshole
        but he swore he hadn't & really
I couldn't be sure I was right
        & every time I doubted
him after that he reminded me
        I'd been wrong once before until
I gave up caring
        about what was true & what wasn't
true so long as I had my bat in my
        bed & my ticket out of
Hartford & I made it & now Kenny
        says that me not having breakfast
with him was what really
        made him know he had to get sober
so he still doesn't know that
        the truth is I never
wanted him to get sober like nobody
        really wants any of us to get sober
they just want to take
        the scarier ride one time & be gone.

 Samuel Amadon is the author of the poetry collection *Like a Sea* (University of Iowa Press, 2010). His poems have appeared or are forthcoming in *American Poetry Review*, *A Public Space*, *Boston Review*, *The New Yorker*, *Ploughshares*, *Tin House*, and elsewhere. He has received fellowships and scholarships from the Bread Loaf Writers' Conference and the Fine Arts Work Center in Provincetown. He lives in Houston.